An A-Maze-ing Colorful Journey Back in Time

HISTORY
Mystery Mazes

Roger Moreau

Sterling Publishing Co., Inc.
New York

This book is dedicated to West, Beth, and Joe.

6   8   10   9   7   5

Published by Sterling Publishing Co., Inc.

387 Park Avenue South, New York, NY 10016

© 2004 by Roger Moreau

Distributed in Canada by Sterling Publishing

c/o Canadian Manda Group, 165 Dufferin Street,

Toronto, Ontario, Canada M6K 3H6

Distributed in Great Britain and Europe by Chris Lloyd at Orca Book

Services, Stanley House, Fleets Lane, Poole BH15 3AJ, England

Distributed in Australia by Capricorn Link (Australia) Pty. Ltd.

P.O. Box 704, Windsor, NSW 2756, Australia

Printed in China
08/09

Sterling ISBN-13: 978-1-4027-1171-8

ISBN-10: 1-4027-1171-9

For information about custom editions, special sales, premium and

corporate purchases, please contact Sterling Special Sales

Department at 800-805-5489 or specialsales@sterlingpub.com.

Contents

Suggested Use of This Book

As you work your way through the pages of this book, try not to mark them. This will enable you to experience these adventures over and over again and will also give your friends a chance to see if their courage and skills match yours.

Special Warning: Even if the way looks too difficult, avoid the temptation to start at the end and work your way backwards. This technique is considered a violation of the rules and could result in your being disqualified.

Cover Maze: See if you can get to *Apollo 11* before it blasts off for the first moon landing. The engines have already started. Find a clear path around this montage of historical events. Better hurry!

Introduction

Throughout time, many events have taken place that could qualify as having historical significance. Such things as natural disasters, wars, inventions, discoveries, and so on could fall into that category. These are the kinds of events that stand out above the average everyday experiences of our lives, affecting the entire world or, at the very least, large numbers of people, for better or worse.

To single out historical events for a selection is not easy. Natural disasters and wars are definitely historical events, but they result in destruction, suffering, and death. They are the type of events we would like to forget and wish had never happened. They cast an ugly shadow over the face of the earth that does not go away. And too often we are reminded of them because of their historical significance. These kinds of historical events have been purposely left out of this book.

The historical events depicted in the following pages, for the most part, celebrate the great accomplishments of humankind. In some cases, they helped expand our understanding of the world; in other cases, they improved the quality of our lives. Even the sinking of the *Titanic*, as tragic as that was, led to greater safety requirements for travel on the sea. You will have a chance to be part of these events. For some events, you will be able to help out where the opportunity presents itself. Other events are more controversial because the exact circumstances are open to dispute. For these, you should record all details, to clear up any mystery. Whatever happens, don't give up if the going gets difficult. This is an opportunity for you to be a part of history.

Historical Facts

Johannes Gutenberg invented the printing press around 1450. His invention lead to a surge in intellectual knowledge at the end of the Middle Ages. The printing press made inexpensive printing possible, so books could be available to a larger number of people. What civilization gained from Gutenberg's invention is beyond calculation. Thanks to other inventors, such as Benjamin Franklin, Alexander Graham Bell, and Thomas Edison, electricity, the telephone, and the lightbulb are everyday conveniences. Think of the flying machine invented by the Wright brothers and the development of mass production using the assembly line by Henry Ford for his Model T car. Because of these inventions, transportation was improved and changed forever for the average person.

Courageous explorers have also left their mark on history. Columbus's voyages, Peary's and Amundsen's treks to the poles, Lindberg's flight across the Atlantic, Hillary's and Norgay's ascent of Mount Everest, the descent of the bathyscaphe *Trieste*, and the flights to the moon during the Apollo missions have brought mankind a better understanding not only of the world, but of the universe. The opening of the Suez Canal in 1869 and the Panama Canal in 1914, along with the completion of the transcontinental railroad in 1869, aided in this transformation.

Discoveries have been important. The discovery of the Rosetta Stone enabled translators to read Egyptian hieroglyphics, and finding King Tut's tomb added to a greater appreciation of the glories and wonders of ancient Egypt. The discovery of gold opened America's west, and that of a vaccine for polio by Jonas Salk saved the lives of thousands of people.

While there have been many other remarkable achievements, the ones on the following pages are significant historical events that would be at the top of any list. Enjoy being a part of them.

The Printing Press

In 1450, Johannes Gutenberg invented the printing press. He is ready to make his first print. Help him by carrying the paper to the press. Find a clear path.

The Voyage of Columbus

In 1492, Christopher Columbus set out on his voyage of discovery. Help each ship, the *Nina*, the *Pinta*, and the *Santa Maria*, find a separate route to the New World. Avoid the waves.

Electricity

In 1752, Benjamin Franklin made his historic kite test that proved lightning is electricity. Repeat his test to calculate lightning's power. Find a path to the gauge connected to the kite being hit by lightning.

Start

Signing of the Declaration of Independence

The Declaration of Independence was signed in 1776. Get your signature on it by finding a clear path to the signing table.

Start

End

The Rosetta Stone

The Rosetta Stone was discovered in 1799 in the town of Rosetta, Egypt. An inscription on the stone resulted in the translation of Egyptian hieroglyphics. Find a clear path to the stone.

Start

End

The Gold Rush

In 1848, James Marshall's discovery of gold at Sutter's Mill in California led to the famous Gold Rush. See if you can find gold.

Start

End

The Transatlantic Cable

The transatlantic cable was laid in 1866. It is going to be destroyed if you don't do something about it. Find a clear path (you can cross over the cable) and take out the octopus.

End

The Transcontinental Railroad

The date is 1869 in Promontory, Utah, and the railroad will be completed when the last golden spike is put into place. Find a clear path, and you can be the one to finish the job.

Start

End

The Suez Canal

It is 1869, and the Mediterranean Sea is about to be joined to the Red Sea as a result of digging the Suez Canal. Take a stick of dynamite and place it in the hole to blow up the final dirt barrier. Better hurry, because someone has already lit the dynamite.

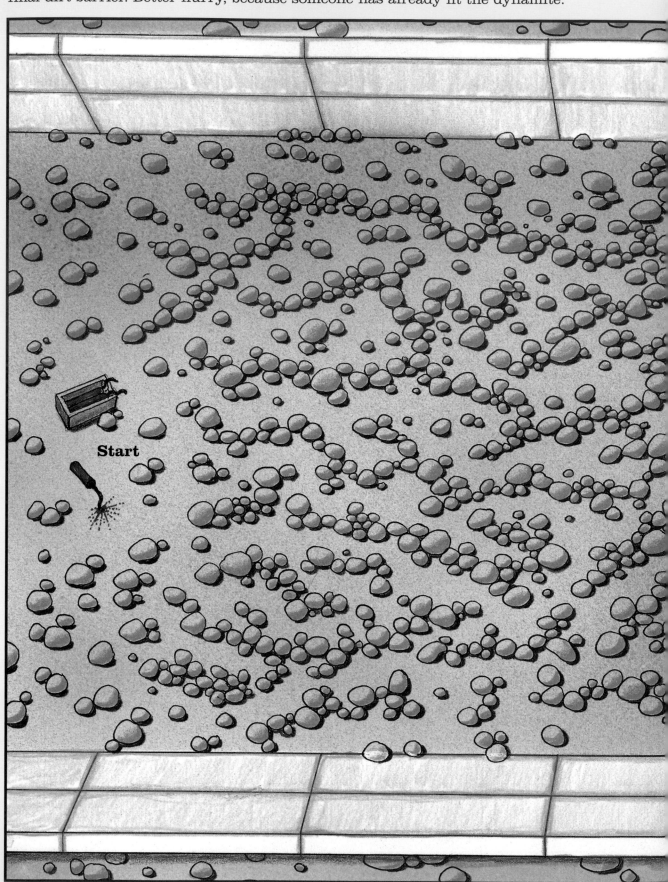

Start

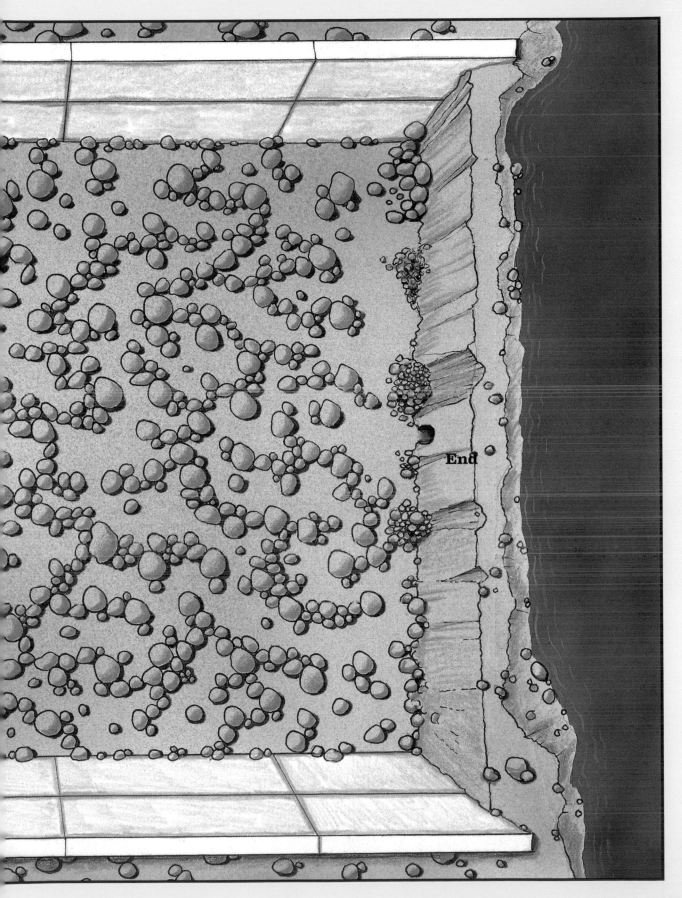

End

The First Telephone

It is 1876, and Alexander Graham Bell is ready to test the telephone. Only one phone is hooked to the electrical cords. Which one is it? Place the number of the correct phone in the box.

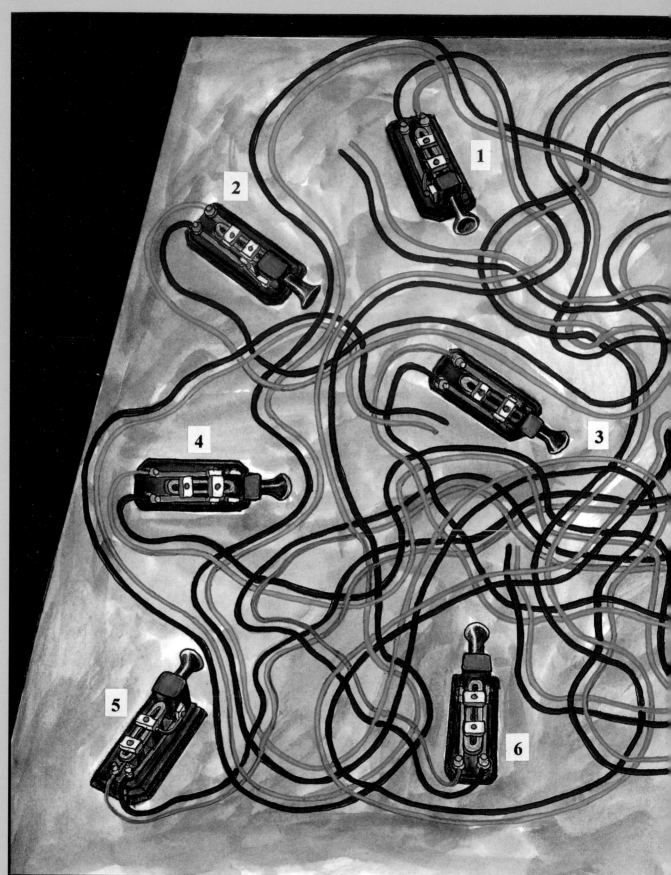

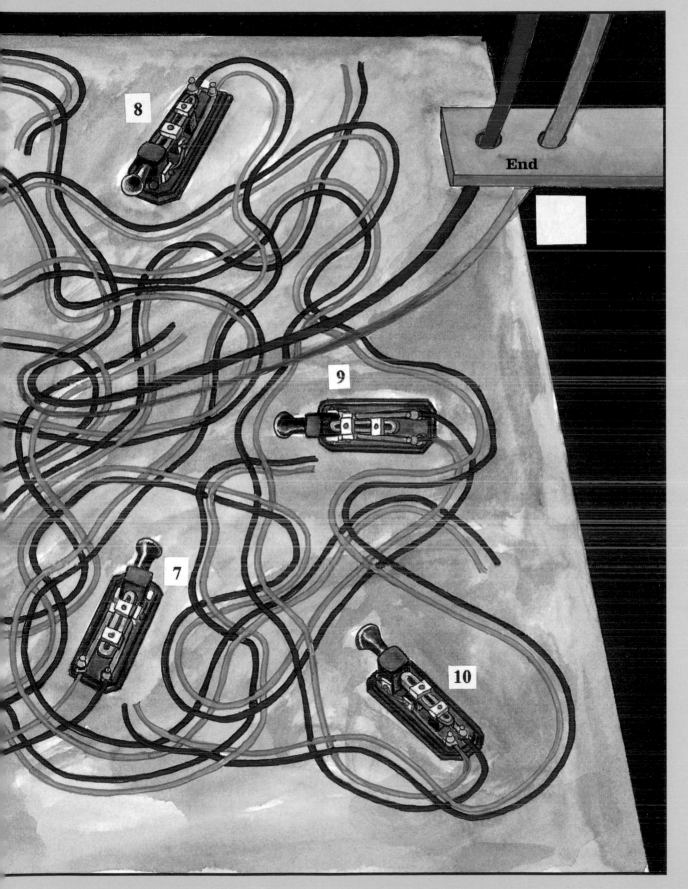

End

The Brooklyn Bridge

It is 1883 and the Brooklyn Bridge, linking the two great cities of Brooklyn and New York, has been completed. Start on the left side and find a clear path across to the right. Only one starting point will get you across. Which one is it?

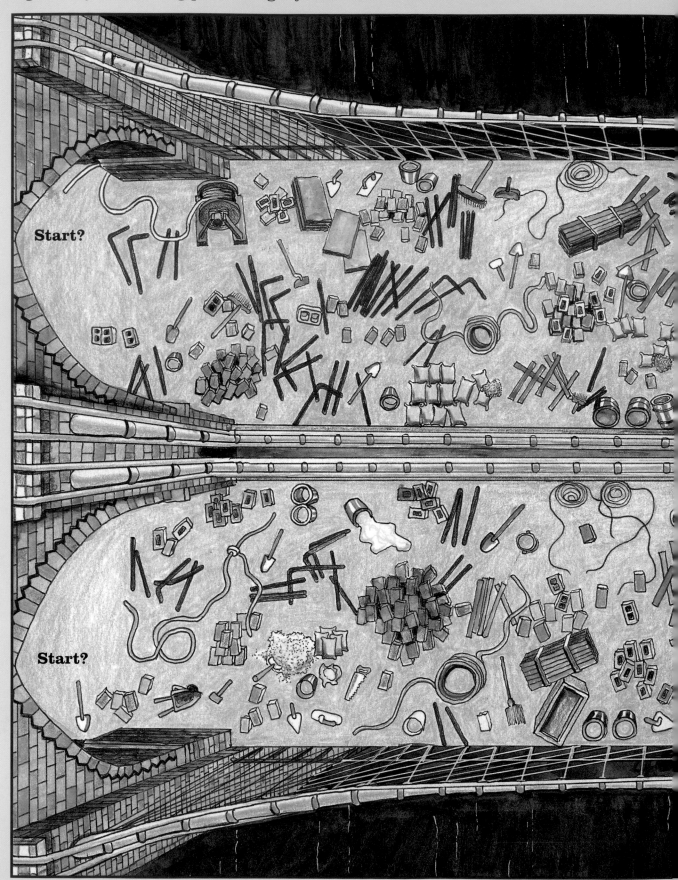

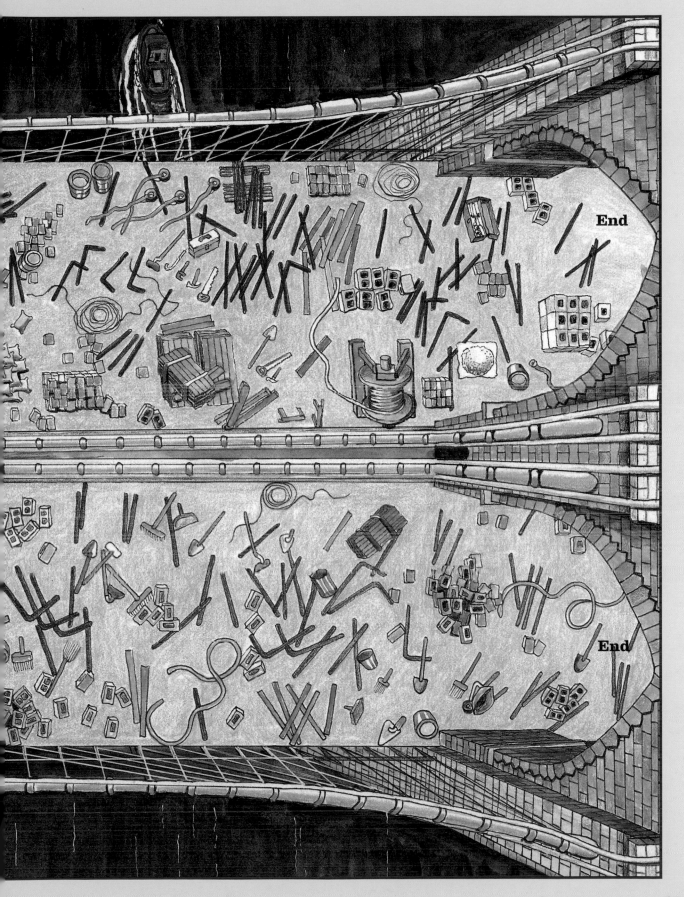

End

End

The Electric Lightbulb

In 1879, Thomas Edison invented the electric lightbulb. Which one is hooked up properly? Trace the cords to find out which bulb is connected.

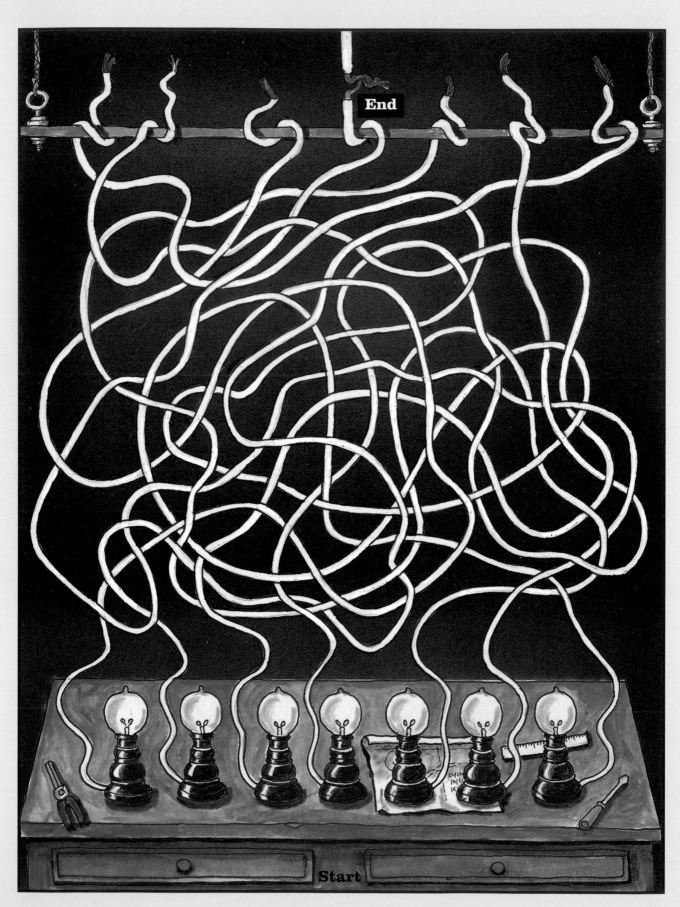

The First Flying Machine

In 1903, the Wright brothers made their first flight in a heavier-than-air machine at Kitty Hawk, North Carolina. Help them put the propeller on the Flyer by finding a clear path from the shop to the engine.

The First Flight

Guide the Flyer away from the air turbulence to the landing spot 852 feet away.

Start

End

The First Transatlantic Flight

Charles Lindbergh was the first to fly solo nonstop across the Atlantic in his plane, the *Spirit of Saint Louis*, in 1927. Help him find the way. Avoid the clouds.

Start

End

33

To the Moon

It's 1969, and *Apollo 11* is on its way to the moon for the first landing. Help the astronauts Neil Armstrong, Edwin Aldrin, and Michael Collins find their way. Advance to the moon through the openings in the grid.

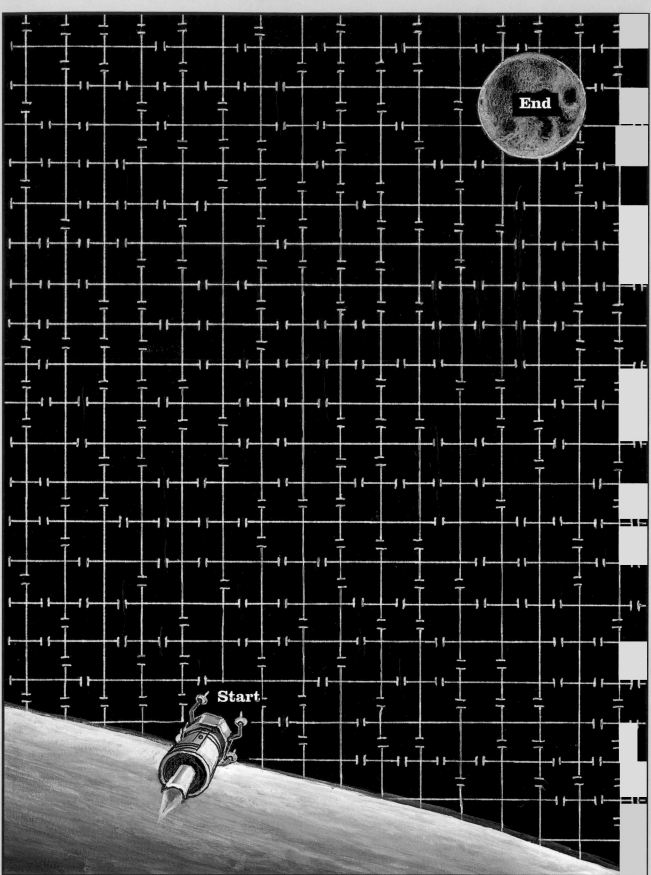

Tranquility Base Ahead

Apollo 11 must land at a spot named Tranquility Base. Help the astronauts by finding the way through the openings in the grid to the landing spot.

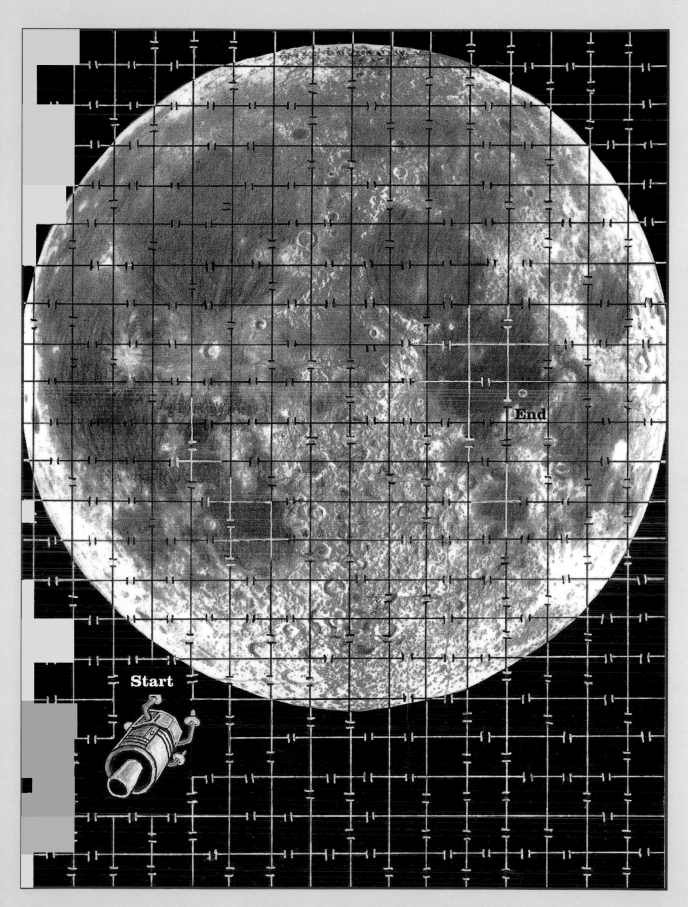

The *Eagle* Has Landed

Now that the lunar module, named *Eagle*, has landed, help the astronauts plant the flag in that open spot. Avoid disturbing any of the rocks.

The *Titanic*

In 1912, the great ship *Titanic* struck an iceberg and sank. Here she is. You can help guide her around the icebergs. If you're not careful, she could end up sinking . . . again.

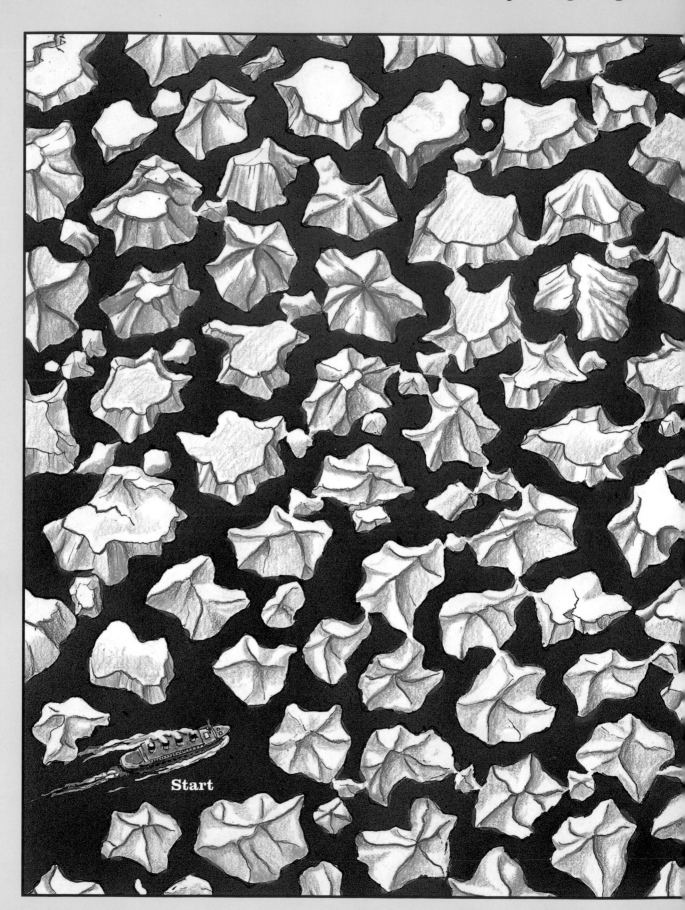

Start

End

Ford's Model T

The use of the assembly line for the mass production of cars by Henry Ford was a great breakthrough, because it meant that almost anyone could own a car. In 1909, the Model T was mass produced. Fill the car radiators with water. Make sure that car

Start
on any
hose

#1 gets filled first, then #2, and so on. Put the car number in the box by the appropriate hose outlet.

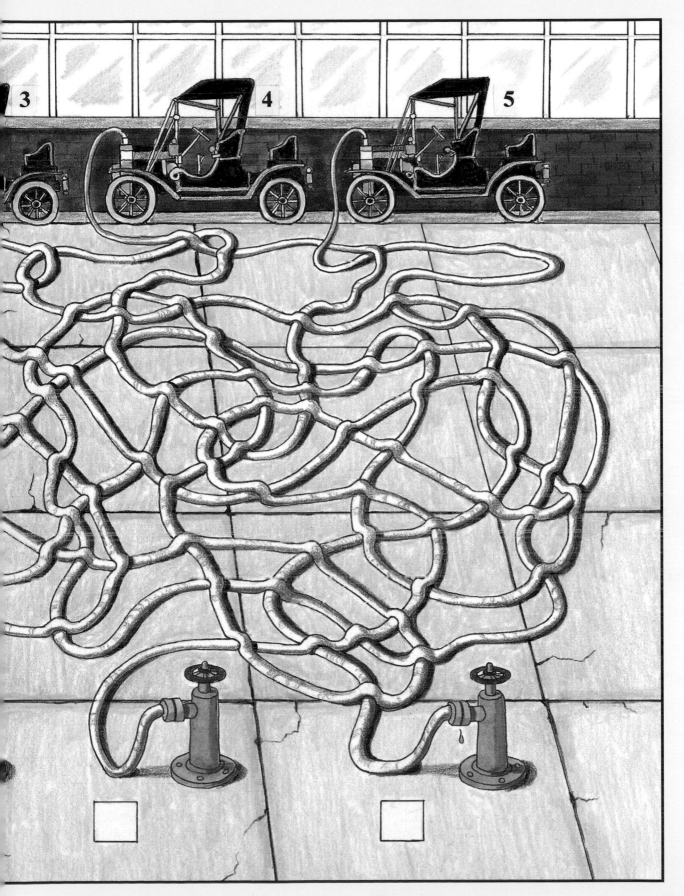

The Panama Canal

The Panama Canal connected the Pacific Ocean to the Atlantic through the Isthmus of Panama in 1914. One of the big dangers was malaria, caused by mosquitoes. Find your way from this dredger to the mosquito swatters, to help fight the problem.

The North Pole

In 1909, Robert Peary reached the North Pole. Join the Pole team by finding a path around the cracks.

The South Pole

In 1911, Roald Amundsen reached the South Pole. Find a clear path and join the South Pole team.

End

Start

The Highest Point on Earth

In 1953, Edmund Hillary and Tensing Norgay reached the highest point on Earth, the summit of Everest, at 29,035 feet. If you hurry, you can get in the photo with Norgay. Avoid the crevasses.

Start

End

The Deepest Spot on Earth

In 1960, the bathyscaphe *Trieste* dove to a depth of 35,800 feet in the Marian Trench in the Pacific Ocean, the deepest spot on earth. Find a clear path to the bottom.

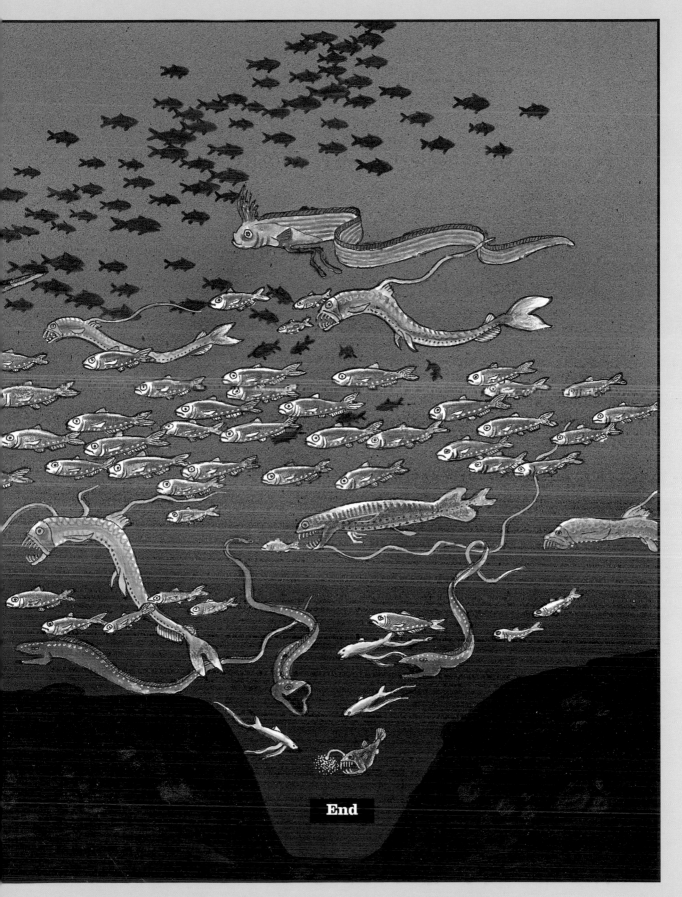

End

King Tut's Tomb

Howard Carter discovered King Tut's tomb in 1923. Find your way to the tomb. It is blocked by stones. You can remove up to six stones to get to the tomb. Good luck.

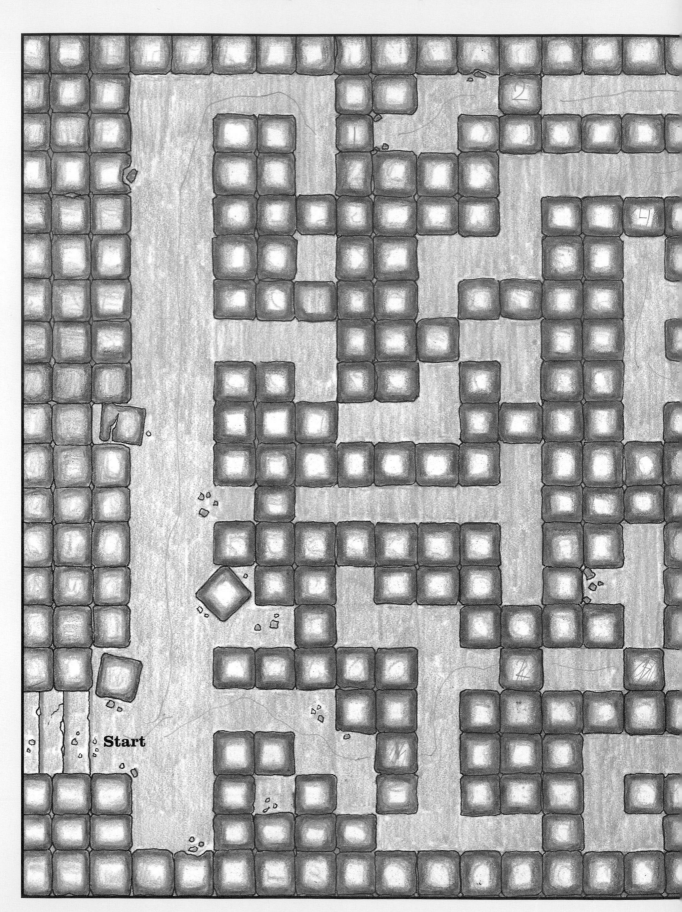

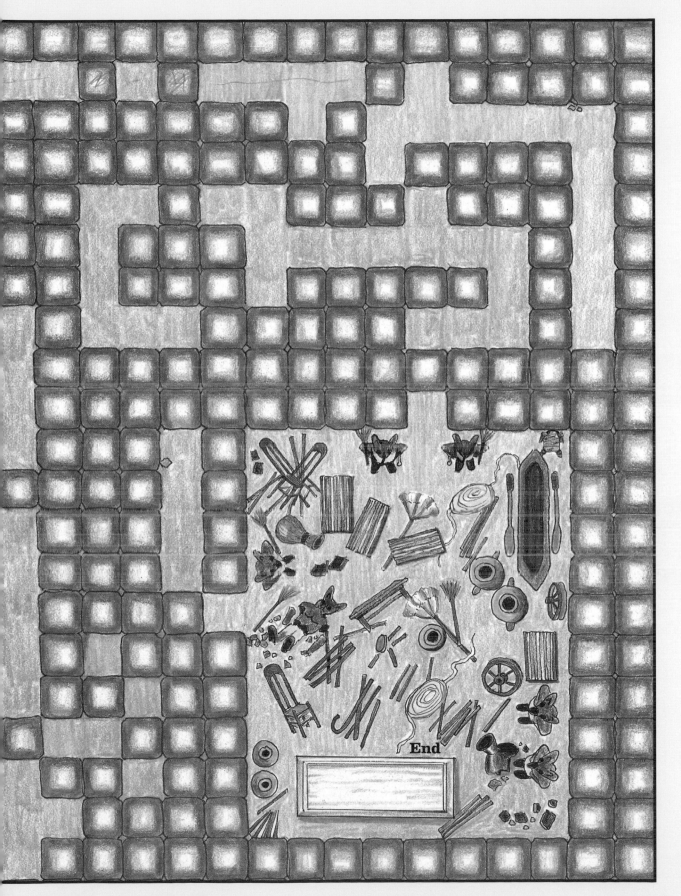

End

No More Polio

In 1955, the antipolio Salk vaccine was pronounced safe, which ended infantile paralysis. Help Jonas Salk with his vaccine by finding the two test tube chemicals that will go into the beaker on the table. Put the numbers in the boxes.

Congratulations!

The above photograph of you with Tensing Norgay on the summit of Mount Everest is proof of your success in the selected historical events in this maze book. As with any important endeavor, the way is not always easy, and there can be a tendency to give up. Those who give up fail, and alter the course of their own personal history and possibly the history of humankind. As you have learned from your experiences in this book, history was made and humankind benefited from people who did not give up. You are that kind of person. It is very possible that one day, in your future, humankind will benefit and history will be made by something you do.

If you had trouble along the way, check the solutions to the mazes on the following pages.

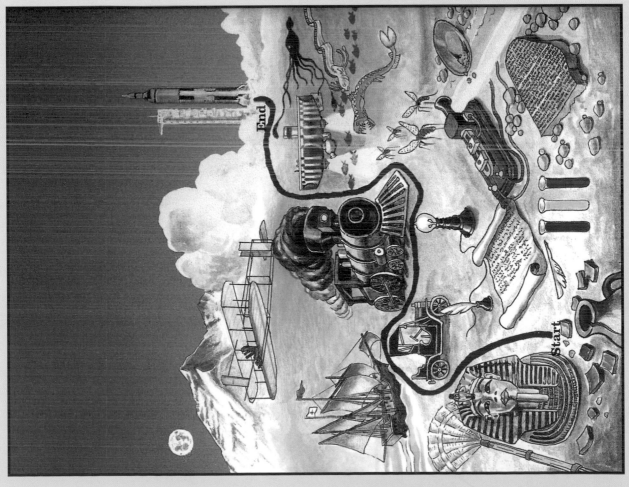

The Voyage of Columbus

End

Start

Start

Start

Electricity

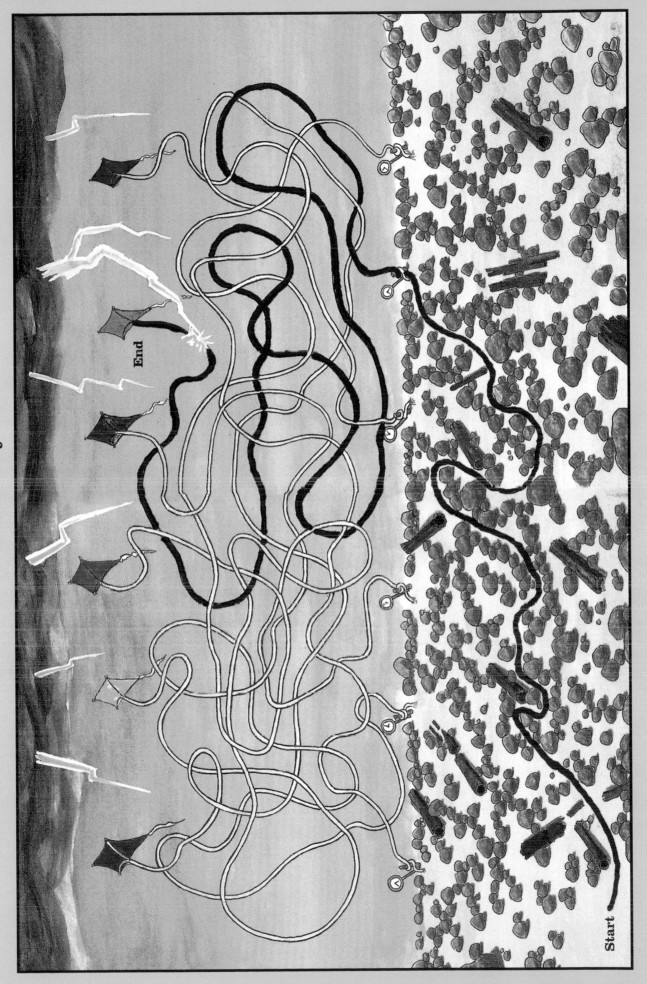

Signing of the Declaration of Independence

Start

End

The Rosetta Stone

The Gold Rush

End

Start

The Transatlantic Cable

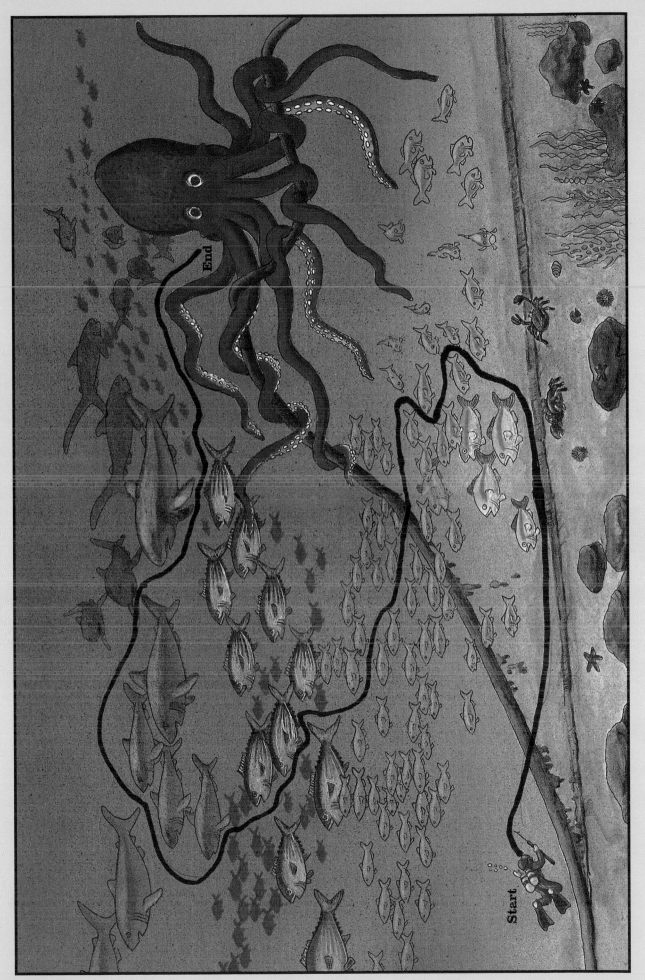

The Transcontinental Railroad

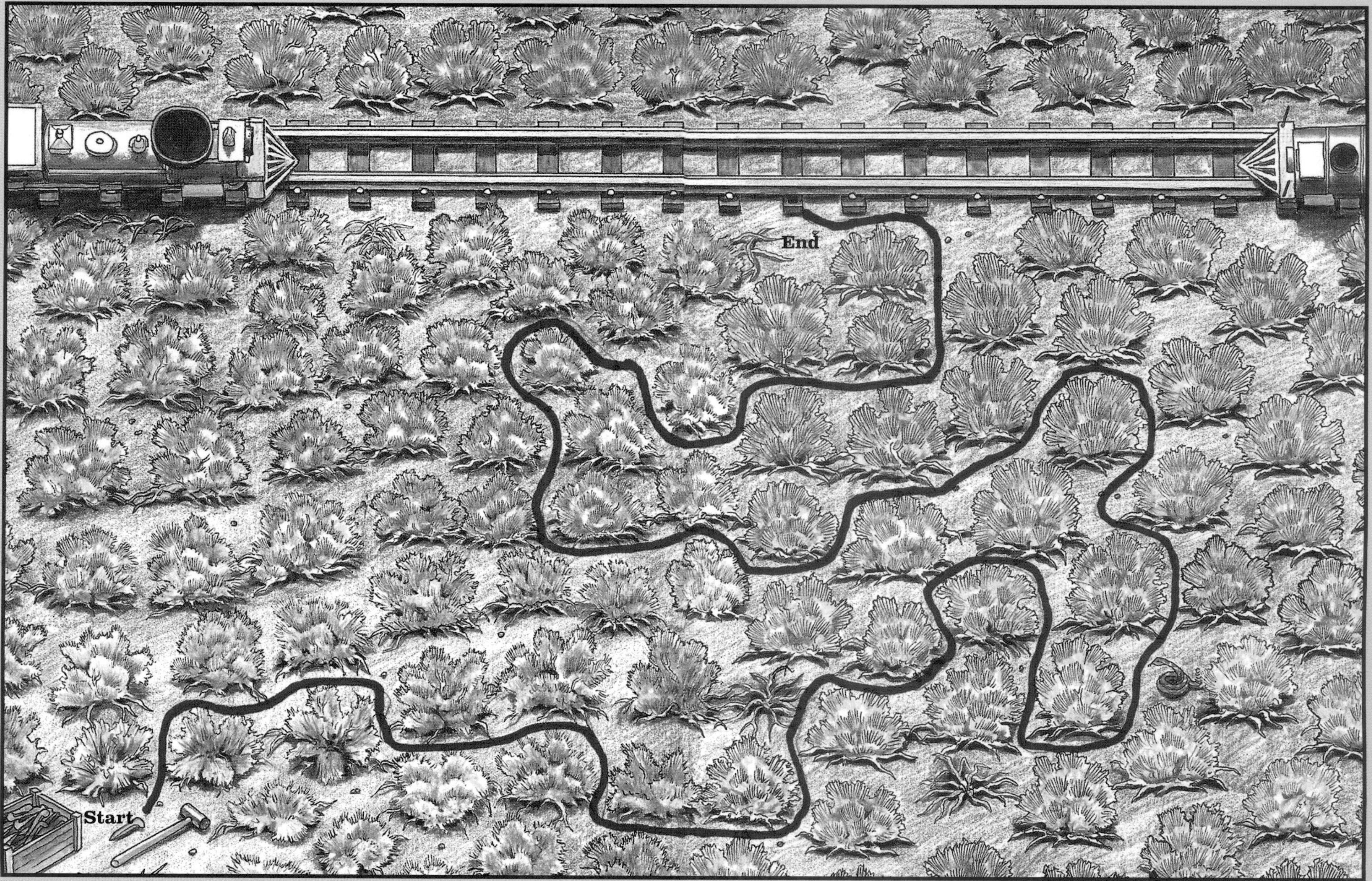

End

Start

The Suez Canal

End

Start

61

The First Telephone

End

7

62

The Brooklyn Bridge

End

Start

The Electric Lightbulb

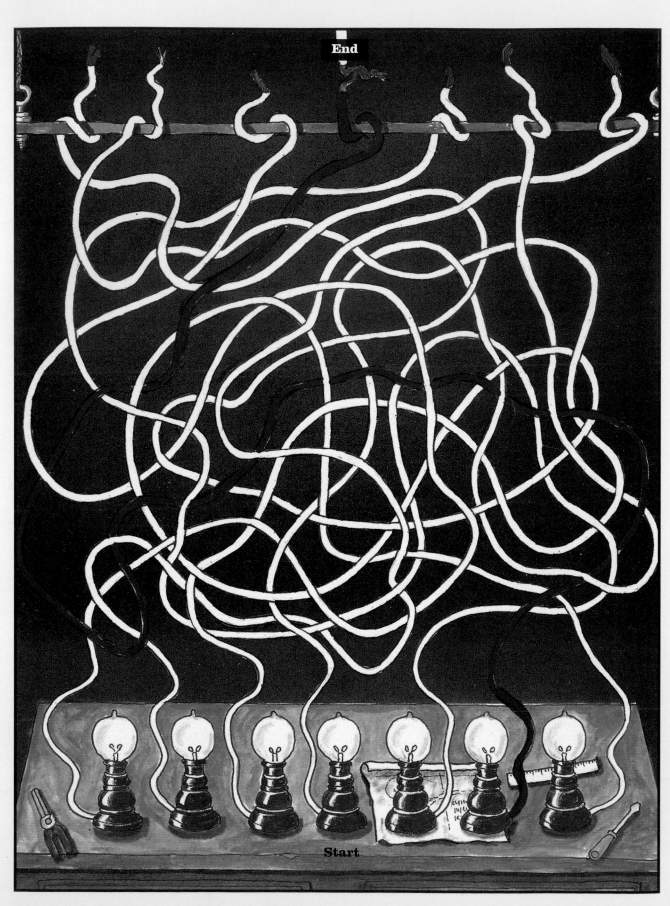

64

The First Flying Machine

The First Flight

The First Transatlantic Flight

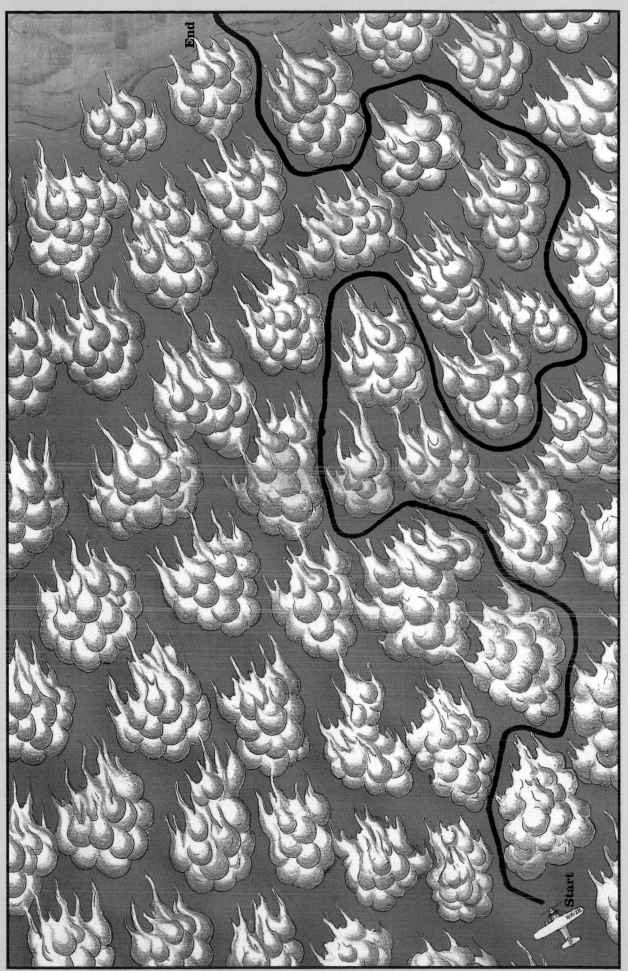

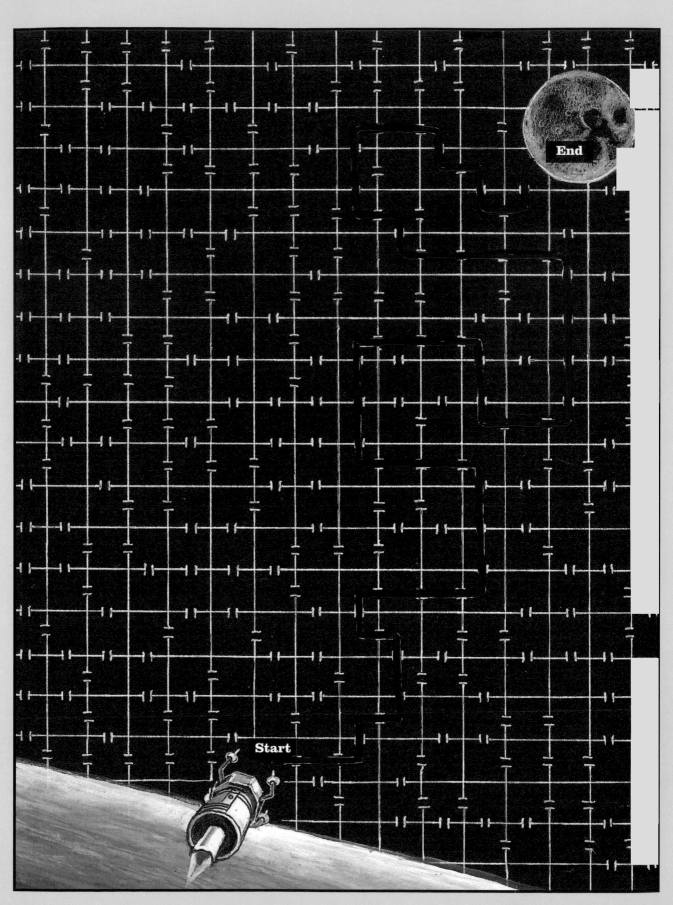

Tranquility Base Ahead

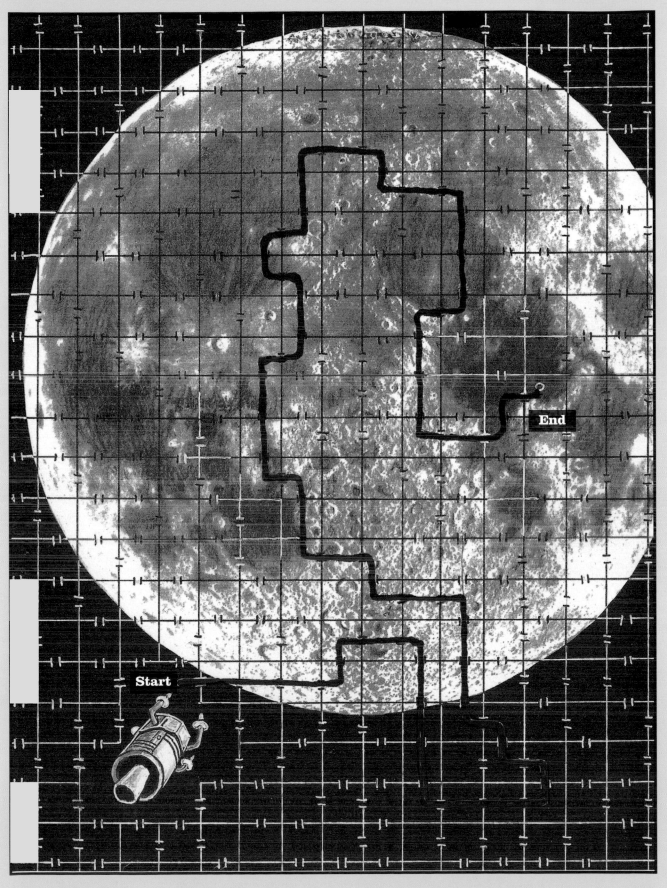

The *Eagle* Has Landed

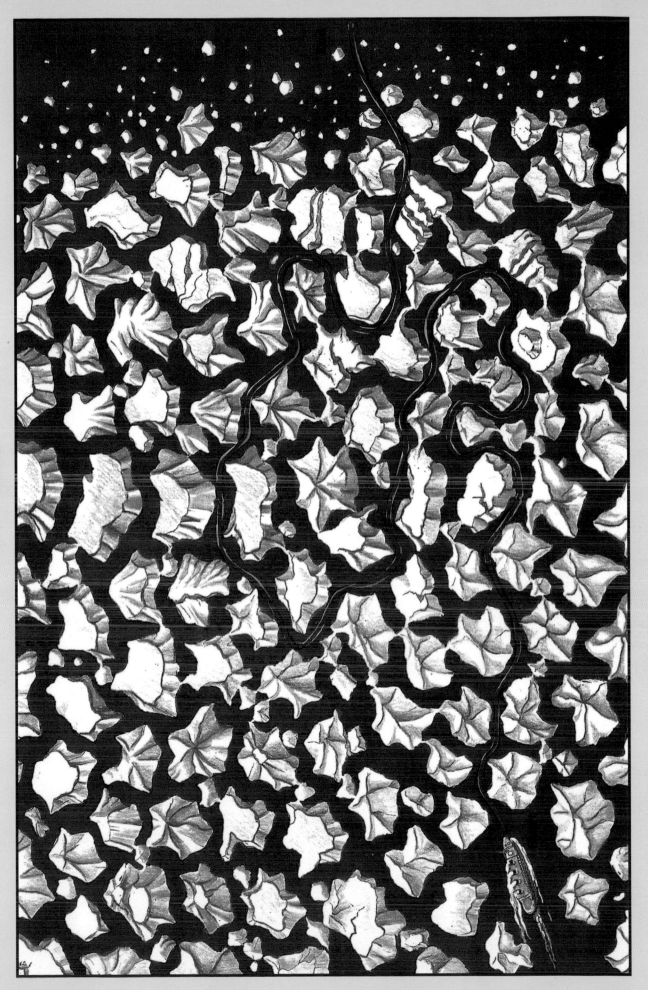

The Titanic

Ford's Model T

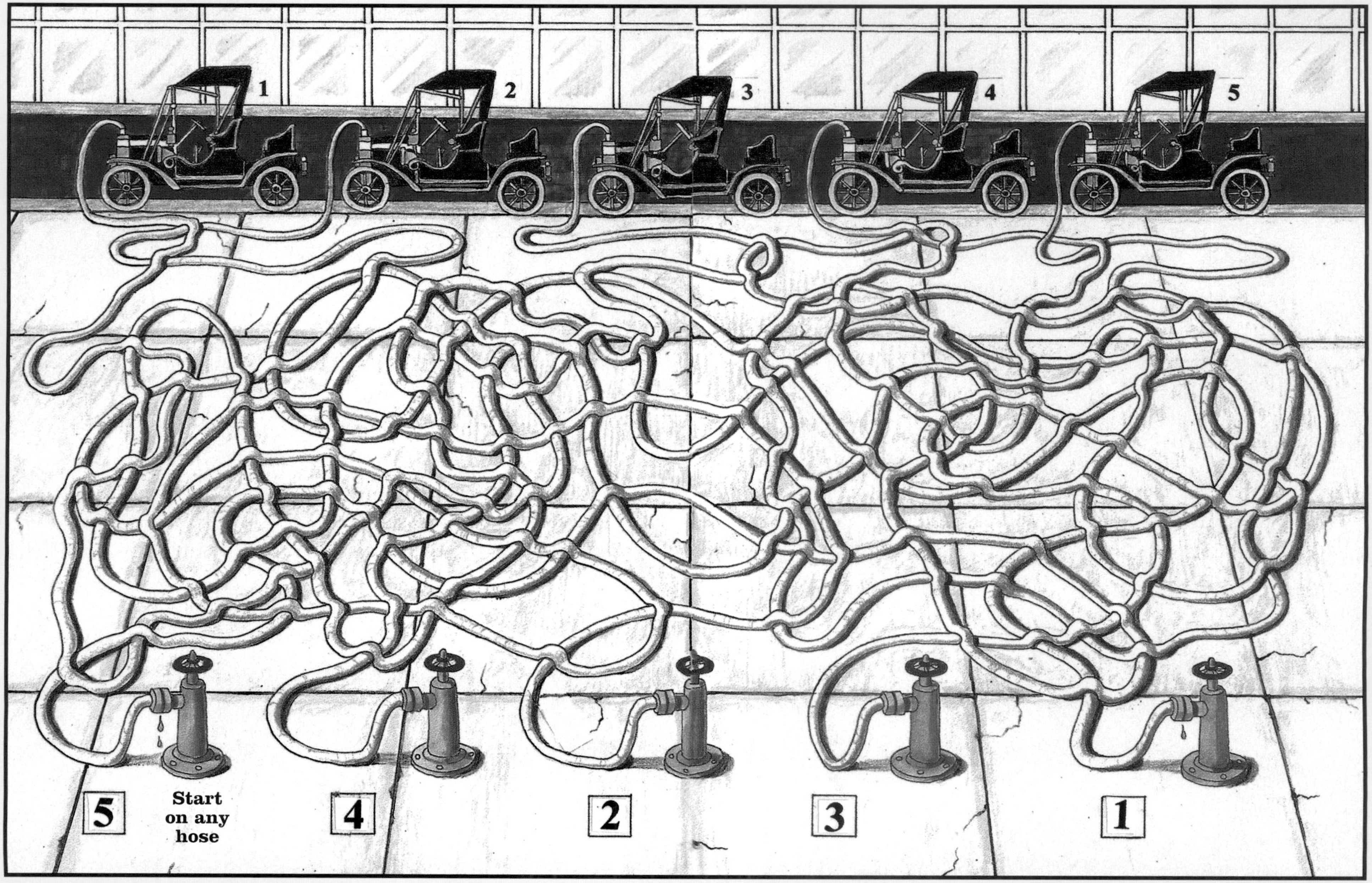

1

3

2

4

5

Start on any hose

72

The Panama Canal

The North Pole

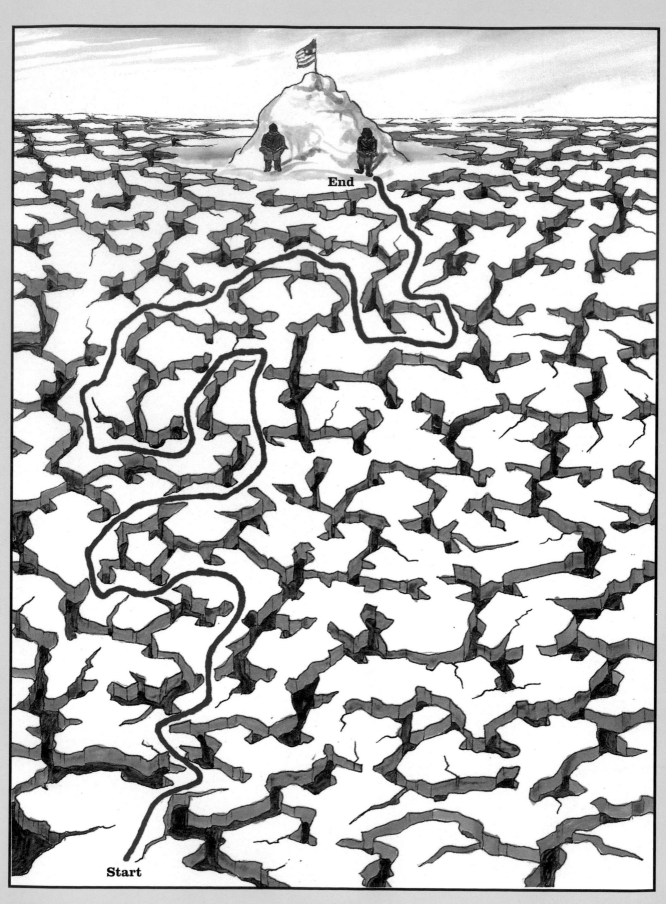

Start

End

The South Pole

The Deepest Spot on Earth

Start

End